TOP HIGH SCHOOL SPORTS
BASKETBALL

A Crabtree Branches Book

THOMAS KINGSLEY TROUPE

CRABTREE
Publishing Company
www.crabtreebooks.com

School-to Home-Support for Caregivers and Teachers

This high-interest book is designed to motivate striving students with engaging topics while building fluency, vocabulary, and an interest in reading. Here are a few questions and activities to help the reader build upon his or her comprehension skills.

Before Reading:
- *What do I think this book is about?*
- *What do I know about this topic?*
- *What do I want to learn about this topic?*
- *Why am I reading this book?*

During Reading:
- *I wonder why...*
- *I'm curious to know...*
- *How is this like something I already know?*
- *What have I learned so far?*

After Reading:
- *What was the author trying to teach me?*
- *What are some details?*
- *How did the photographs and captions help me understand more?*
- *Read the book again and look for the vocabulary words.*
- *What questions do I still have?*

Extension Activities:
- *What was your favorite part of the book? Write a paragraph on it.*
- *Draw a picture of your favorite thing you learned from the book.*

TABLE OF CONTENTS

TO THE HOOP!	4
Basketball History	6
Basketball Season	8
High School Basketball Teams	10
Rules of the Game	12
Equipment & Uniform	14
Basketball Positions	16
Defense Type: Man to Man	20
Defense Type: Zone	22
Fouls and Free Throws	24
Tournaments and Playoffs	26
Conclusion	28
Glossary	30
Index	31
Websites to Visit	31
About the Author	32

TO THE HOOP!

You jump straight up to tip the ball back to your teammate. You **dribble** toward the hoop as the opposing team tries to swat the ball away. You fake to the left and move right, tricking your defender. The ball is passed to you. You pivot, aim, and sink a perfect basket. Two points!

Lace up your shoes and get a good stretch in. We're about to learn why basketball ranks among the...TOP HIGH SCHOOL SPORTS.

FUN FACT

Basketball is the only American sport that didn't originate in another country.

BASKETBALL HISTORY

James Naismith

James Naismith was a physical education teacher in Springfield, Massachusetts. In 1891, he invented a game that could be played during the long winter months. He attached two peach baskets to the balconies inside a **gymnasium**.

FUN FACT
Basketball was introduced as a high school sport in 1905.

Players were challenged to throw the ball into the basket to score points. From there, the game of basketball was born!

After a "basket" was made, someone had to bring a ladder to retrieve the ball so everyone could keep playing. Years later, an open-ended net was attached to the hoop to make it easier to retrieve the ball.

BASKETBALL SEASON

In most high schools, basketball season starts in the late autumn and is played through the early winter. Since basketball is played indoors, it can be played in any kind of weather. Rain or snow? Game on!

Like many sports played at the high school level, basketball is played by both boys and girls.

The first high school girl's basketball game was played in 1896. It featured Chicago Austin High School squaring off against Oak Park High School.

The first high school boy's basketball game was played in 1893, 14 months after James Naismith invented the game. The game was played between Morgan Park Academy and the West Side YMCA in Chicago.

HIGH SCHOOL BASKETBALL TEAMS

Most high schools have four basketball teams. They have a varsity team for boys and a varsity team for girls. Varsity teams typically are made up of the school's stronger athletes.

To give players who aren't quite at the varsity level a chance to play, junior varsity teams are formed.

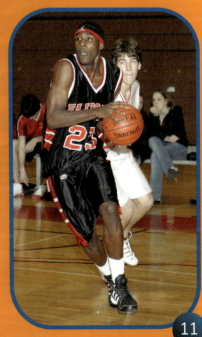

FUN FACT

Smaller schools who don't have enough players might opt for a co-ed team, where boys and girls play on the same team.

RULES OF THE GAME

In basketball, five players from each team score points by making baskets. Each basket is worth two points. Free throws are worth one point. The players move the ball across the court by bouncing, or dribbling the ball.

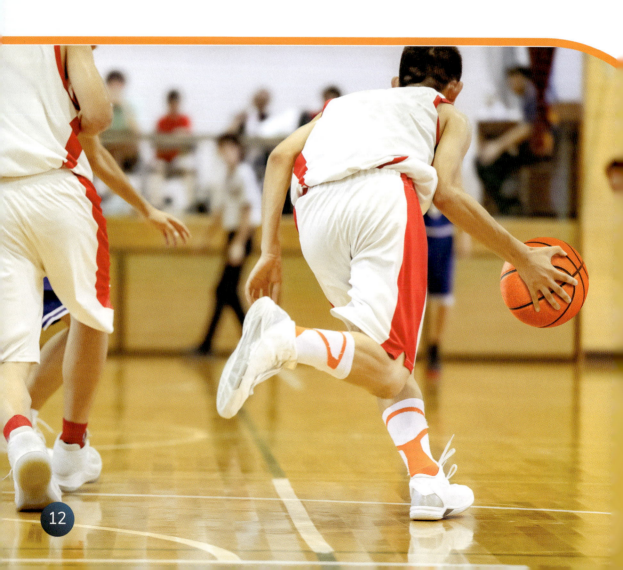

High school basketball games are played in four 8-minute **periods**. The team with the most points at the end of the 4th period wins.

FUN FACT

3-point shots were added into high school basketball in 1987.

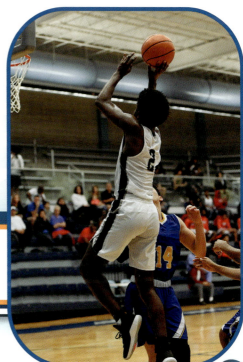

EQUIPMENT & UNIFORM

High school basketball games are played indoors on a court with hoops and backboards attached on each end. The most important piece of equipment is the basketball itself!

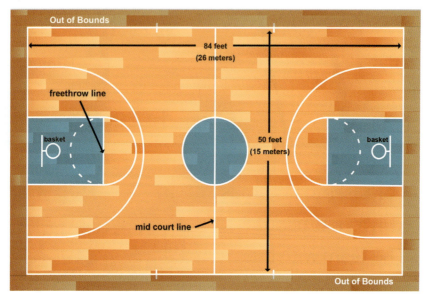

FUN FACT

High school girls' basketball teams use a slightly smaller ball. It measures 28.5 to 29 inches (72.3 to 73.6 cm) in circumference and weighs 18 to 20 ounces (0.51 to 0.56 kg). Boys' teams use 29 to 30 inch (73.6 cm to 76.2 cm) balls that weigh 20 to 22 ounces (0.56 to 0.62 kg).

Basketball players wear shorts and a jersey with the team's name, **logo**, player's last name and number on them. Scuff-free basketball shoes are used to race up and down the court.

Sometimes the referees need to signal a player's number to the sidelines if there's a foul or violation. Because they can't show any number higher than 5 with one hand, the numbers 6, 7, 8, and 9 are usually not used in basketball.

BASKETBALL POSITIONS

When the team has the ball, they are on **offense**. Offensive players work together to dribble the ball closer to the basket. They pass the ball to an open player who can shoot and score.

Point guard – Often the shortest, but the best ball-handler on the team. They are often the team leader while on the court.

Shooting guard – The team's best outside shooter. They need to be good at dribbling and passing the ball.

Small forward – The second or third best shooter. They need to be fast and able to shoot up close and from the outside.

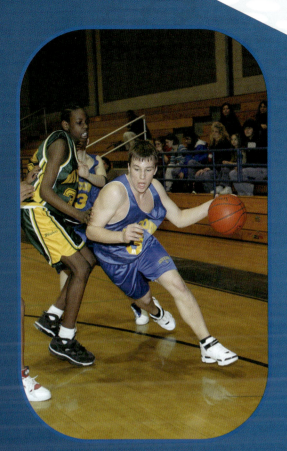

SMALL FORWARD

POINT GUARD

When the team loses control of the ball, they are on **defense**. Defensive players work together to keep the offense from scoring baskets.

Power forward – These players are usually second tallest. They should be able to score from close to mid-range.

Center – Usually the tallest player on the team. They are often positioned under the basket to block the ball or rebound.

Bench – The players not on the court. They are often called in to give other players a break. The players who are swapped out become part of the bench.

BENCH

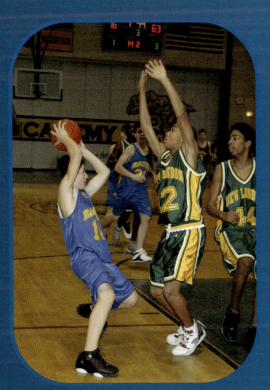

POWER FORWARD

FUN FACT

In the early days of basketball, the ball wasn't dribbled. Instead, players had to throw it from wherever it was caught. A team at Yale University in Connecticut was credited for advancing the ball by dribbling in 1897.

DEFENSE TYPE: MAN TO MAN

There are two types of defense used in high school basketball. The first is man-to-man defense. In man-to-man defense, a defensive player is assigned to an offensive player. They will stay with the player to try to block or steal the ball.

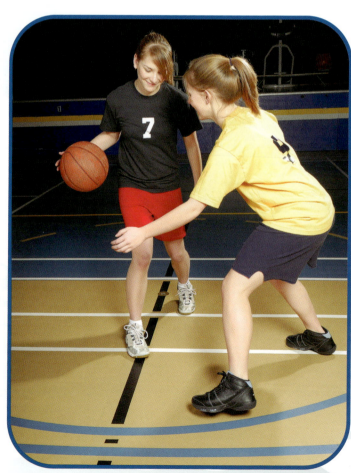

This defensive style is considered better for helping high school athletes develop basketball skills.

> **FUN FACT**
>
> Almost all professional basketball teams utilize man-to-man defense.

DEFENSE TYPE: ZONE

In zone defense, players are assigned spots on the court to act as a shield for incoming offensive players. They protect their space to keep the ball away from their basket.

A 2-3 zone defense places two players at the front and three at the back. This protects the key, the area below and in front of the basket, where most shots are made.

FUN FACT

Basketball was included in the Olympics for the first time in Berlin, German in 1936.

FOULS AND FREE THROWS

Basketball has many rules. Double-dribbling or being out of bounds are common **violations**. They will cause the ball to be turned over to the other team.

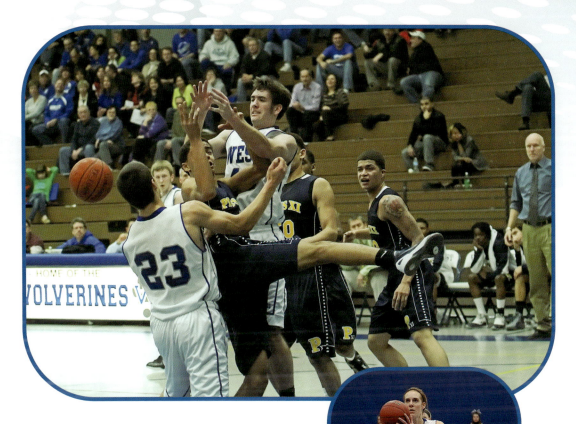

Physical **fouls** on a player who is shooting usually result in a free throw. A free throw is granted from the free throw line inside the top of the key. The player can take a shot without a defensive player interfering.

There are penalties for rough play! The referee will keep track of how many fouls are called on a player. If a player commits five fouls during a high school basketball game, they're considered "fouled out." They get to spend the rest of the game on the bench!

TOURNAMENTS AND PLAYOFFS

High school basketball teams compete with other schools to find out who's the best. Many schools participate in playoffs and championship **tournaments**.

Teams are broken into classes, based on the total number of students in the high school. This means smaller schools face off against smaller schools. This allows high schools of all sizes to complete fairly!

CONCLUSION

Basketball is one of the most exciting sports high-schoolers play today. The sport takes speed, **precision**, and teamwork to sink game-winning baskets. There's a reason the stands are packed with cheering fans.

Will you lace up your shoes and take a shot at making the high school team? Maybe you can become the next big star. With practice and patience, you'll see why basketball is considered one of the TOP HIGH SCHOOL SPORTS!

GLOSSARY

defense (DEE-fenss): defending a goal against the opposing team

dribble (DRIB-uhl): continuous bouncing of a basketball

foul (FOUL): interference in an opponent's playing

gymnasium (jim-NAY-zee-uhm): a room equipped for games or physical exercise

logo (LOH-goh): a symbol or design to identify a team

offense (AW-fenss): the team possessing the ball in an attempt to score

periods (PIHR-ee-uhdz): lengths of time in a sports game

precision (pri-SIJH-uhn): exact or accurate

tournament (TUR-nuh-muhnt): a series of contests or games played between competing teams

violations (vye-uh-LAY-shuhnz): breaking of rules

INDEX

court 12, 14, 15, 16, 18, 22
defense 18, 20, 21, 22, 23
dribble(d) 4, 16, 19
free throw(s) 12, 24, 25
fouls 24, 25
Naismith, James 6, 9
offense 16, 18
playoffs 26
points 4, 7, 12, 13
varsity 10, 11

WEBSITES TO VISIT

https://www.ducksters.com/sports/basketball.php

https://www.sikids.com/basketball

https://kids.kiddle.co/Basketball

ABOUT THE AUTHOR

Thomas Kingsley Troupe

Thomas Kingsley Troupe is the author of a big ol' pile of books for kids. He's written about everything from ghosts to Bigfoot to third grade werewolves. He even wrote a book about dirt. When he's not writing or reading, he gets plenty of exercise and remembers sacking quarterbacks while on his high school football team. Thomas lives in Woodbury, Minnesota with his two sons.

Written by: Thomas Kingsley Troupe
Designed by: Jennifer Dydyk
Edited by: Kelli Hicks
Proofreader: Ellen Rodger

Photographs: Cover background pattern (and pattern throughout book © HNK, basketball on cover and title page © EFKS, cover photos of players © Monkey Business Images, Page 4 © dotshock, Page 5 bottom photo © taka1022, Page 7 © AlexanderZam, Page 9 background photo © hxdbzxy, Page 10 © Debby Wong, Page 11 bottom photo © Larry St. Pierre, Page 12 © taka1022, Page 13 top photo © Monkey Business Images, bottom photo © JoeSAPhotos, Page 14 diagram © Kashtanowww, Page 17 photos © Larry St. Pierre, illustrations © Alesandro14, Page 19 top photo © Monkey Business Images, bottom photo © Larry St. Pierre, Page 20 © Lorraine Swanson, Page 21 © taka1022, Page 27 © Ramosh Artworks, All images from Shutterstock.com except: Page 5 bottom photo, Page 8, Page 11 top photo © Monkey Business Images | Dreamstime.com, Page 14 photo © Sports Images | Dreamstime.com, Pages 15, 22, 23, 24, 25, 26, 28, 29 © Louis Horch | Dreamstime.com. Page 6 photos and Page 9 top photo courtesy of the Library of Congress

Library and Archives Canada Cataloguing in Publication

CIP available at Library and Archives Canada

Library of Congress Cataloging-in-Publication Data

CIP available at Library of Congress

Crabtree Publishing Company
www.crabtreebooks.com   1-800-387-7650

Printed in the U.S.A./CG20210915/012022

Copyright © 2022 **CRABTREE PUBLISHING COMPANY**

All rights reserved. No part of this publication may be reproduced, stored in a retrieval system or be transmitted in any form or by any means, electronic, mechanical, photocopying, recording, or otherwise, without the prior written permission of Crabtree Publishing Company. In Canada: We acknowledge the financial support of the Government of Canada through the Canada Book Fund for our publishing activities.

Published in the United States
Crabtree Publishing
347 Fifth Avenue, Suite 1402-145
New York, NY, 10016

Published in Canada
Crabtree Publishing
616 Welland Ave.
St. Catharines, Ontario L2M 5V6